Edgar Allan Poe's Pie

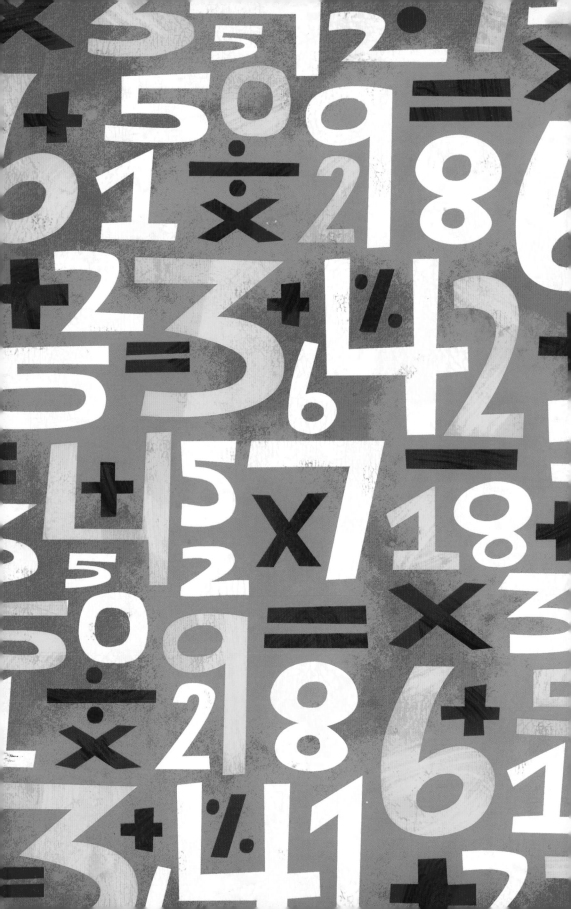

J. Patrick Lewis + Illustrated by Michael Slack

Edgar Allan Poe's Pie

MATH PUZZLERS

IN CLASSIC POEMS

HOUGHTON MIFFLIN HARCOURT

BOSTON   NEW YORK

To the memory of the poets
whose poems I have parodied
—J.P.L.

For my lovely little Lily—M.S.

For information about permission to reproduce selections
from this book, write to trade.permissions@hmhco.com or to
Permissions, Houghton Mifflin Harcourt Publishing Company,
3 Park Avenue, 19th Floor, New York, New York 10016.

www.hmhco.com

The illustrations in this book were digitally painted
and collaged in Photoshop. The text type was set in
Better Type Right and Joppa. The display type was
set in Joppa.

The Library of Congress has cataloged the hardcover
edition as follows:
Lewis, J. Patrick.
Edgar Allan Poe's pie : math puzzlers in classic poems
/ written by J. Patrick Lewis ; illustrated by Michael
H. Slack.
p. cm.

1. Mathematics—Juvenile poetry. 2. Children's poetry,
American. 3. American poetry—Adaptations. 4. English
poetry—Adaptations. 5. Mathematical recreations—
Juvenile literature. I. Slack, Michael H., 1969– ill.
II. Title.
PS3562.E9465E34 2012
811'.54—dc23
2011025735

ISBN: 978-0-547-51338-6 hardcover
ISBN: 978-0-544-45612-9 paperback

Manufactured in China
SCP 10 9 8 7 6 5 4 3
4500610977

Contents

Edgar Allan Poe's Apple Pie

INSPIRED BY "THE RAVEN" BY EDGAR ALLAN POE

Once upon a midnight rotten,
Cold, and rainy, I'd forgotten
All about the apple pie
Still cooling from the hour before.
I ignored the frightful stranger
Knocking, knocking . . . I, sleepwalking,
Pitter-pattered toward the pantry,
Took a knife from the kitchen drawer,
And screamed aloud, "How many cuts
Give me ten pieces?" through the door,
      The stranger bellowed, "Never four!"

ANSWER: Cut the apple pie across 5 times to make 10 equal slices.

9

Edward Lear's Elephant with Hot Dog

INSPIRED BY "THERE WAS AN OLD MAN WITH A BEARD" BY EDWARD LEAR

When an elephant sat down to order
A half of a third of a quarter
Of an eighty-foot bun
And a frankfurter, son,
Was it longer than three feet, or shorter?

ANSWER: $\frac{1}{2}$ x $\frac{1}{3}$ x $\frac{1}{4}$ = $\frac{1}{24}$;
$\frac{1}{24}$ x 80 feet = $3\frac{1}{3}$ feet;
$3\frac{1}{3}$ feet is greater than 3 feet, so the hot dog is longer.

Walt Whitman's Web-Covered Shoe

INSPIRED BY "A NOISELESS PATIENT SPIDER" BY WALT WHITMAN

A noiseless patient spider—
I counted her filaments, first one, then two, then dozens,
Counted one hundred and forty, unreeling out of her until
A wind gust blew sixty percent of them off
To New Jersey. That left . . . oh, who can say how many
Trembling strands remained?

Can you, spider watcher, tell me the magic number?
What if a bigger, fatter spider-bully crawled in and shooed away
The little shoe spider, then built his own arch bridge by adding
Ninety more filaments to the smaller arachnid's mansion?

O-MY SOLES™

ANSWER: 60% x 140 = 84 filaments blew away.
140 − 84 = 56 filaments remained from the first spider.
Then the bully spider added 90 filaments.
So 56 + 90 = 146 filaments from both spiders combined.

Emily Dickinson's Telephone Book

INSPIRED BY "MY LIFE CLOSED TWICE BEFORE ITS CLOSE" BY EMILY DICKINSON

My book closed twice before its close—
The two opposing pages
That added up to 113—
Were smudged around the edges—

At noon I opened it again—
When waking—from my slumbers.
The phone book so befuddles me—
What were those two page numbers?

ANSWER: 113 ÷ 2 = 56.5;
rounding 56.5 up and down =
pages 56 and 57.

Lewis Carroll's Fish and Chips

INSPIRED BY "YOU ARE OLD, FATHER WILLIAM" BY LEWIS CARROLL

"You are old, Father William," the young man said,
  "And your noggin resembles a gourd.
Do you know that your body's attached to your head,
  Where the marbles are usually stored?"

"In my youth," Father William replied, "I could chew
  Fish and chips while I added large sums,
Like forty, eighteen, thirty-six, minus two. ①
  Oh, how happy it made dads and mums."

"You are old," said the lad, "and your hat is too tight.
  That's so simple a child could get it.
What can you expect doing sums by flashlight
  And fish and chips math? Extra credit?"

"In my youth," said the sage, "I discovered the key:
  If I ate fish and chips, I could say
What remained after nineteen divided by three. ②
  'Twas remarkably easy that way."

"You are old," said the youth, "and your mind is a sieve,
   A perfectly pointless utensil.
You've ignored every piece of advice I could give.
   I fear there's no lead in your pencil."

"In my youth," said his father, now red in the face,
   "When I ate fish and . . . Oh, never mind.
Any fraction—one-ninth?—the right decimal place ③
   You could count on yours truly to find."

"You are old," said the youth, "so I'm bound to assume
   That whatever you say is absurd.
But must you tut-tuttingly strut through the room
   With a nest on your head for a bird?"

"Now I gave you three puzzles. A word to the wise—
   Pay attention and follow my lips.
For arithmetic brilliance, a father's surprise:
   Stop the studying—eat fish and chips."

ANSWERS: ① 40 + 18 + 36 − 2 = 92; ② 19 ÷ 3 = 6, remainder 1; ③ ¹/₉ = 0.11111

17

Hilaire Belloc's Crackerjack Yak

INSPIRED BY "THE YAK" BY HILAIRE BELLOC

As a friend to the children, I recommend Yak,
  For the Yak always says what he means
And he means what he says. He's as sharp as a tack,
  Although the old boy's full of beans.

In Tibet he is noble, so no one will scoff
  At a Yak. He's the favorite son.
If you ask a Yak what he weighs, he will cough
  (One cough is twice more than a ton).

What's a yard of a Yak (the whole herd)? He coughs back
  Sixteen and a half in a row.
Now once he has coughed up the yard of Yak,
  He'll *reyak* like a wild buffalo!

Robert Frost's Boxer Shorts

INSPIRED BY "STOPPING BY WOODS ON A SNOWY EVENING" BY ROBERT FROST

Whose underwear?! I wish I knew
Who left these for me, all brand-new—
Five dollars, ninety cents a pair.
They're not my size. I'm forty-two.

And fourteen pairs? Why, I could share
A few with you with some to spare.
If nine are cotton (cotton blend)
And five are silk, then let's compare:

On each set, how much did he spend?
Arithmetic is just the friend
To multiply, divide, or add.
And what's the total in the end?

These boxer shorts are not half bad
With lions, tigers, stripes, and plaid.
My tightie whities look so sad.
My tightie whities look so sad.

Eleanor Farjeon's Math Sub

INSPIRED BY "W IS FOR WITCH" BY ELEANOR FARJEON

I met a wizened woman,
And she was skin and bones.
She said, "I'll be your sub today.
I'm Mrs. Numerical Jones."
Some kid yelled, "Hey, how old are you?"
She smiled and said, "Let's see
If you might know the answer—
Easy as one, two, three.

"I'm twice as old as Jericho,
My cat who turned fourteen.
Now multiply by five, and then
Divide by two. Darlene,
My parakeet, can tell you
How old I am. She speaks!
She's mastered Mrs. Numerical's
Numerical techniques."

Miranda guessed, "You're eighty."
Jorge bellowed, "Eighty-one."
Taniqua shouted, "Sixty-four!"
Oh, we had lots of fun.
When bending over laughing,
How she rattled skin and bones,
Till Artie finally guessed the age
Of Mrs. Numerical Jones.

ANSWER: Mrs. Jones is 2 x 14 = 28, 28 x 5 = 140, 140 ÷ 2 = 70 years old.

A. A. Milne's
Spooky Garden

INSPIRED BY "US TWO" BY A. A. MILNE

Wherever I am, there's always Boo,
Boo in the flowers with me.
The size of our garden is eight by two.
"How much wire for the fence," says Boo,
"If it wraps all around as it ought to do?
Let's guess together," says Boo to me.
"Let's guess together," says Boo.

"What's eight plus two?" I say to Boo.
"That's ten!" Boo says to me.
"But eight plus two will not quite do.
It's eight plus two *times* two," says Boo, ①
"Is how much wire we need for you
To wrap around," says Boo to me.
"To wrap around," says Boo.

"The rimeter?" I say to Boo.
"*Perim*," says Boo to me.
"The area, from a bird's-eye view,
Of a garden plot?" says Boo. ②
"But now we have *two* sums to do.
Let's think together," says Boo to me.
"Let's think together," says Boo.

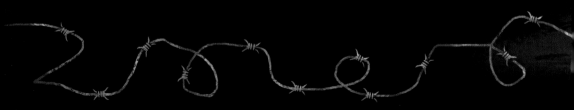

ANSWERS: ① Perimeter = length plus width times two, so 8 feet + 2 feet = 10 feet,
10 feet x 2 = 20-foot perimeter.
② Area = length times width, so 8 feet x 2 feet = 16 square-foot area.

William Carlos Williams's Pizza

INSPIRED BY "THIS IS JUST TO SAY" AND "THE RED WHEELBARROW"
BY WILLIAM CARLOS WILLIAMS

The fifteen-inch square pizza
with three-by-three-inch slices
was so inviting

I couldn't resist
eating nineteen and a half of them

Forgive me, Flossie
you were hungry, too
I put the box back
in the refrigerator

beside the white chickens
how many pieces
of pizza were left?

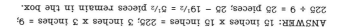

ANSWER: 15 inches x 15 inches = 225; 3 inches x 3 inches = 9;
225 ÷ 9 = 25 pieces; 25 − 19½ = 5½ pieces remain in the box.

Langston Hughes's Train Trip

INSPIRED BY "APRIL RAIN SONG" BY LANGSTON HUGHES

Let the train miss you.
Let the train be late by ten minutes so you can finish your snack.
Let the train steam along like a cloud.

The train ticket costs fourteen dollars, but the tax on
The train ticket is ten percent; then add a tip to the conductor
(Fifteen percent of the ticket plus tax), which you have not got.
So what is the total cost of the train ride?

Ah, I love the train.

ANSWER: 10% = .10

.10 x $14 = $1.40 in tax, so the cost of the ticket is $15.40.
But the tip to the conductor is 15%, so .15 x $15.40 = $2.31.
So the total cost of the train ride is $15.40 + $2.31 = $17.71.

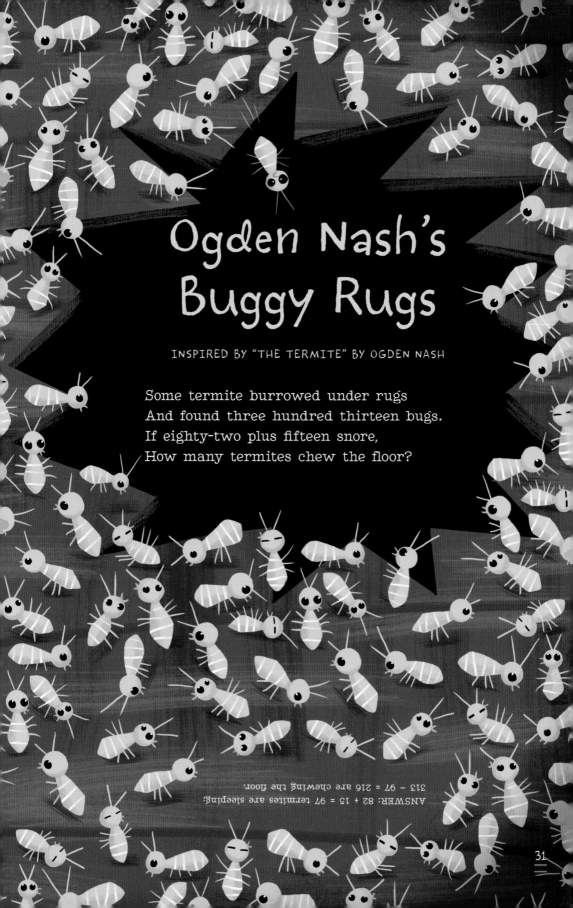

Ogden Nash's Buggy Rugs

INSPIRED BY "THE TERMITE" BY OGDEN NASH

Some termite burrowed under rugs
And found three hundred thirteen bugs.
If eighty-two plus fifteen snore,
How many termites chew the floor?

ANSWER: 82 + 15 = 97 termites are sleeping;
313 − 97 = 216 are chewing the floor.

John Ciardi's Shark Dentist

INSPIRED BY "ABOUT THE TEETH OF SHARKS" BY JOHN CIARDI

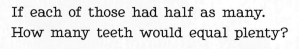

The thing about a shark is—teeth,
Said shark expert my brother Keith.

To study sharks, he happily
Set sail to greet them out at sea.

Keith counted the first pointed row—
Eight hundred twelve! Four rows to go.

If each of those had half as many.
How many teeth would equal plenty?

Before Keith finished adding, he
Was swallowed by shark dentistry.

ANSWER: 812 teeth in one row, 4 x ($^1/_2$ of 812) = 4 x 406 = 1,624 in the other rows,
812 + 1,624 = 2,436 teeth.

ANSWER: 100% = 1, and 4% = .04. If the hippo-po-tah-tum ate 4% of me with each bite, then to eat 100% of me, he must have taken 1 ÷ .04 = 25 bites.

Shel Silverstein's
Hippo-po-tah-tum

INSPIRED BY "BOA CONSTRICTOR" BY SHEL SILVERSTEIN

Oh, I'm being eaten
By a hippo-po-tah-tum
At 4 percent per bite!
He's bitin' my ankles,
Bitin' my toes,
My shins and knees,
Never mind my clothes.
He's bitin' my thighs,
My tummy-tum-tum,
Bitin' my hips.
Ow! He bit my bum,
That hippo-po-tah-tum!
How many bites
From top to bottom
Is enough for a hungry
Hippo-po-tah-tum?

And now some prose about the poets . . .

EDGAR ALLAN POE

(1809–1849): Inventor of the detective-fiction genre, Poe was a master of mystery and gothic tales. His parents died by the time he was three, and Poe's life and death are as shrouded in mystery as his literary work. He is well loved for his short stories, but it is his poem "The Raven" for which he is best remembered.

EDWARD LEAR

(1812–1888): A marvelous landscape and bird painter, Lear became one of the two most famous children's poets of the nineteenth century, the other being Lewis Carroll. He popularized the limerick, and his nonsense verse became a staple for untold numbers of young English readers.

WALT WHITMAN

(1819–1892): The so-called father of free verse, Whitman is among the most influential poets in America. The legacy of his self-published *Leaves of Grass* (1855) still reverberates wherever poetry is prized. Whitman's free-spirited lifestyle would later inspire the beat movement. The poet Ezra Pound called him "America's poet . . . he *is* America."

EMILY DICKINSON

(1830–1886): Born in Amherst, Massachusetts, to a wealthy family, Dickinson led a reclusive life. Fewer than a dozen of her nearly eighteen hundred poems were published during her lifetime, yet she is ranked on the shortlist of major American poets. Her work is distinguished by exquisite description, slant rhyme, and a festival of dashes.

CHARLES LUTWIDGE DODGSON, A.K.A. LEWIS CARROLL

(1832–1898): English author, mathematician, and clergyman, he is the creator of *Alice's Adventures in Wonderland* and *Through the Looking-Glass*. Only Edward Lear was his equal at nonsense verse, as seen in Carroll's poems "Jabberwocky" and "The Hunting of the Snark." His life, like his work, was "curiouser and curiouser."

HILAIRE BELLOC

(1870–1953): The prolific Anglo-French writer and historian Belloc became a British citizen in 1902. A formidable speaker, he rose to become president of the Oxford Union Debating Society and a member of Parliament. His *Cautionary Tales for Children*—humorous poems, each with a dubious moral—were steeped in satire to adult tastes, despite the title.

ROBERT FROST

(1874–1963): Frost personified the rural New England about which he wrote so often. Though he never finished college, Frost was awarded many honorary degrees, won four Pulitzer Prizes for Poetry, and read at the inauguration of John F. Kennedy in 1961.

ELEANOR FARJEON

(1881–1965): Known to her family as "Nellie," Farjeon suffered a childhood of ill health and spent her time in the attic surrounded by books. Her poem "Morning Has Broken" was later turned into a hit song by Cat Stevens. Farjeon went on to win numerous writing awards.

A. A. MILNE (1882–1956):

First published in 1926, Milne's *Winnie-the-Pooh* features a boy, Christopher Robin, named for the author's only son. Though Milne became a noted playwright and children's poet (*When We Were Very Young* and *Now We Are Six*), his later writing was overshadowed by his beloved Pooh bear stories.

WILLIAM CARLOS WILLIAMS (1883–1963):

Williams was a pediatrician as well as a poet. Marianne Moore, another famous poet, wrote that Williams's poems used "plain American which cats and dogs can read." His poem "The Red Wheelbarrow" may be the most imitated poem of the twentieth century.

LANGSTON HUGHES

(1902–1967): Hughes was a leading poet of the Harlem Renaissance (1920s and 1930s). He was a master of vibrant and lyrical poems, such as "The Dream Keeper" and "The Negro Speaks of Rivers." His poems and stories reflect the overwhelming pride he felt about being black in white society.

OGDEN NASH

(1902–1971): Nash's name is synonymous with American humorous verse. His poetic style depended on inspired, wholly unexpected rhymes and puns in lines of differing length and irregular meter. He called himself a "worsifier," but his work was highly regarded in the literary community. In 2002, the United States Postal Service issued an Ogden Nash stamp.

JOHN CIARDI

(1916–1986): In 1959 Ciardi coauthored a book called *How Does a Poem Mean?* on how to read, write, and teach poetry, which became a classic of its kind. Primarily known as a poet and translator of Dante, Ciardi also wrote inspired nonsense verse, such as *The Man Who Sang the Sillies*.

SHELDON ALLAN "SHEL" SILVERSTEIN

(1930–1999): Known as Uncle Shelby, Silverstein was an enormously popular singer-songwriter, cartoonist, and, most famously, children's poet. His books, such as *Where the Sidewalk Ends*, *A Light in the Attic*, *Falling Up*, and *The Giving Tree* have sold millions of copies in many languages.

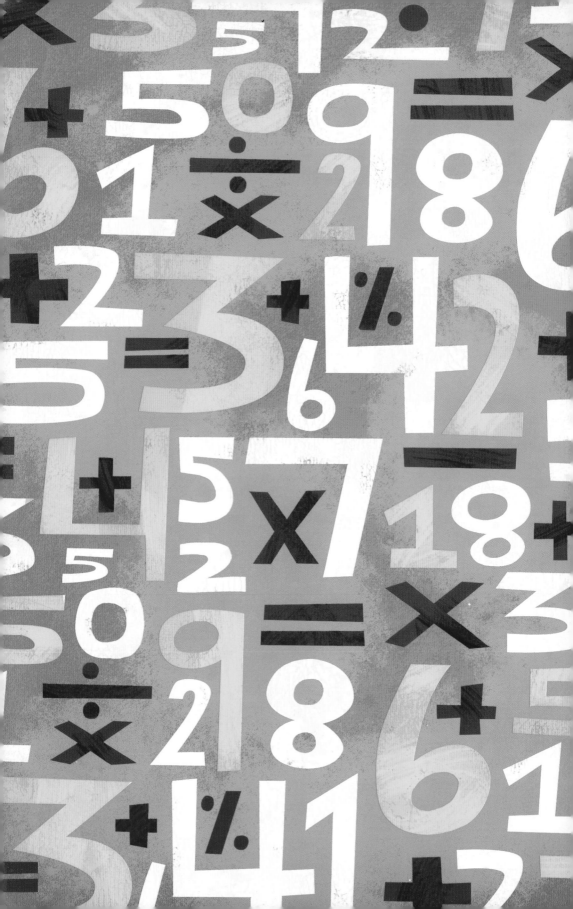